ACTIVITY BOOK

3

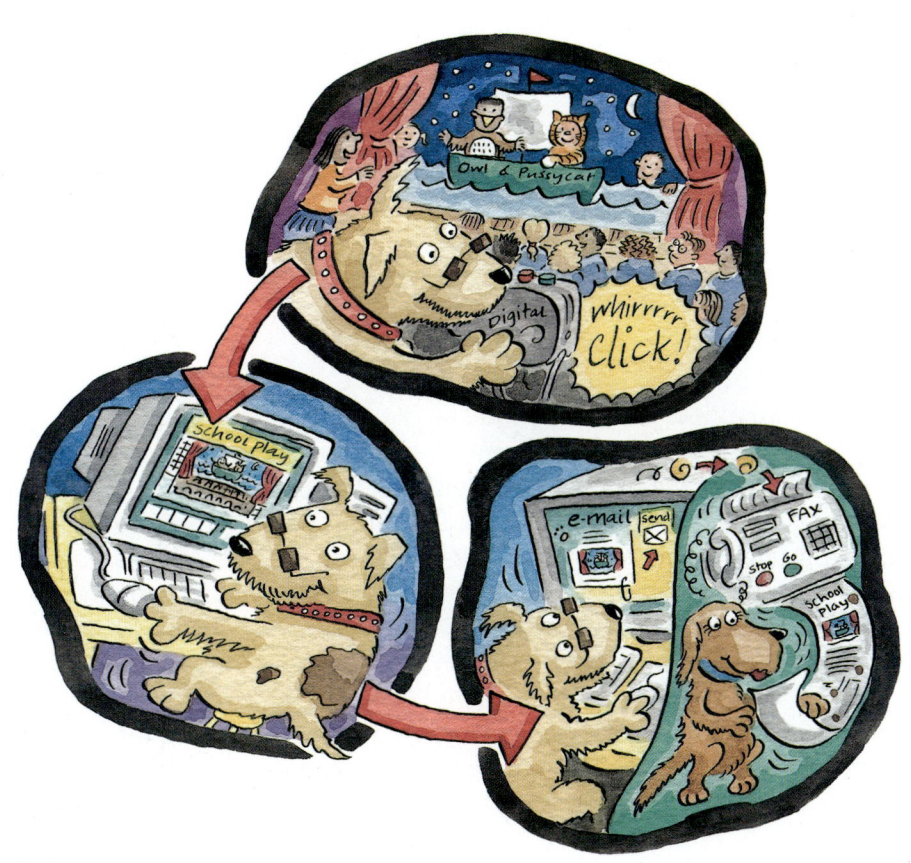

Julianne Aldred and **Nicholas Flesher**

Every effort had been made to trace copyright holders and to obtain their permission for the use of copyright material. The authors and publishers would gladly receive any information enabling them to rectify any error or omission in subsequent editions.

First published 2000

Smart Learning Limited
Sheraton House, Castle Park
Cambridge, CB3 0AX
Tel: 01223 370072 Fax: 01223 370003

Text © Smart Learning Limited

Acknowledgements

Designed by Gecko Limited, Bicester, Oxon
Illustrations commissioned by Karen Homer at Gecko Limited
Editorial work by Anita Clark and Lyn Corson
Consultant: Louis Fidge

Produced by bigtop, Bicester, Oxon
Cover design by Nick Welsh, Mono Industries, Cambridge
Cover illustrations by Beccy Blake

All colour reproduction by Gecko Limited, Bicester, Oxon

Illustrations by Phil Healey – 6 & 7; Beccy Blake – 15, 30; Belthan Mathews c/o Sylvie Poggio – 21, 32, 33, 39 (top right); Tim Davies c/o Sylvie Poggio – 20, 40, 48; Lisa Smith c/o Sylvie Poggio – 18 (bottom), 24, 25, 26 (top), 29 (middle); Sarah Warburton c/o Sylvie Poggio – 12; Barbara Vagmozzi c/o Sylvie Poggio – 52, 53; Jackie Harland – 18 (top), 34, 36, 38 (bottom); Andy Quelch – 16; Martin Ursell c/o Kathy Jakeman illustration – 8; Mark McLaughlin – 46; DTP – Gecko Ltd – 10, 14, 17, 26 (bottom), 27, 28, 29 (top), 38 (top), 39 (top left), 51; Tom Morgan – 42, 44; Phil Healey – 55, 56, 58, 59, 61

All our rights reserved. No part of this publication may be reproduced, stored in a retrieval system, or transmitted, in any form or by any means, electronic, mechanical, photocopying, recording or otherwise, without prior permission of Smart Learning Limited.

British Library Cataloguing-in-Publication Data
A CIP record for this book is available from the British Library

ISBN 1-84276-000-9

Printed in Italy by LEGO SPA, Vicenza

Introduction

This Year 3 Pupil Activity Book:

- Supports the teaching of the ICT national curriculum
- Meets the objectives of the ICT QCA scheme of work
- Is divided into skills units which cover the key topic areas of the QCA scheme of work
- Provides stimulus material for carrying out whole class and teacher-led activities
- Offers an integrated task at the end of each unit, giving opportunities for bringing together the key skills learnt
- Offers assessment opportunities through the integrated tasks set

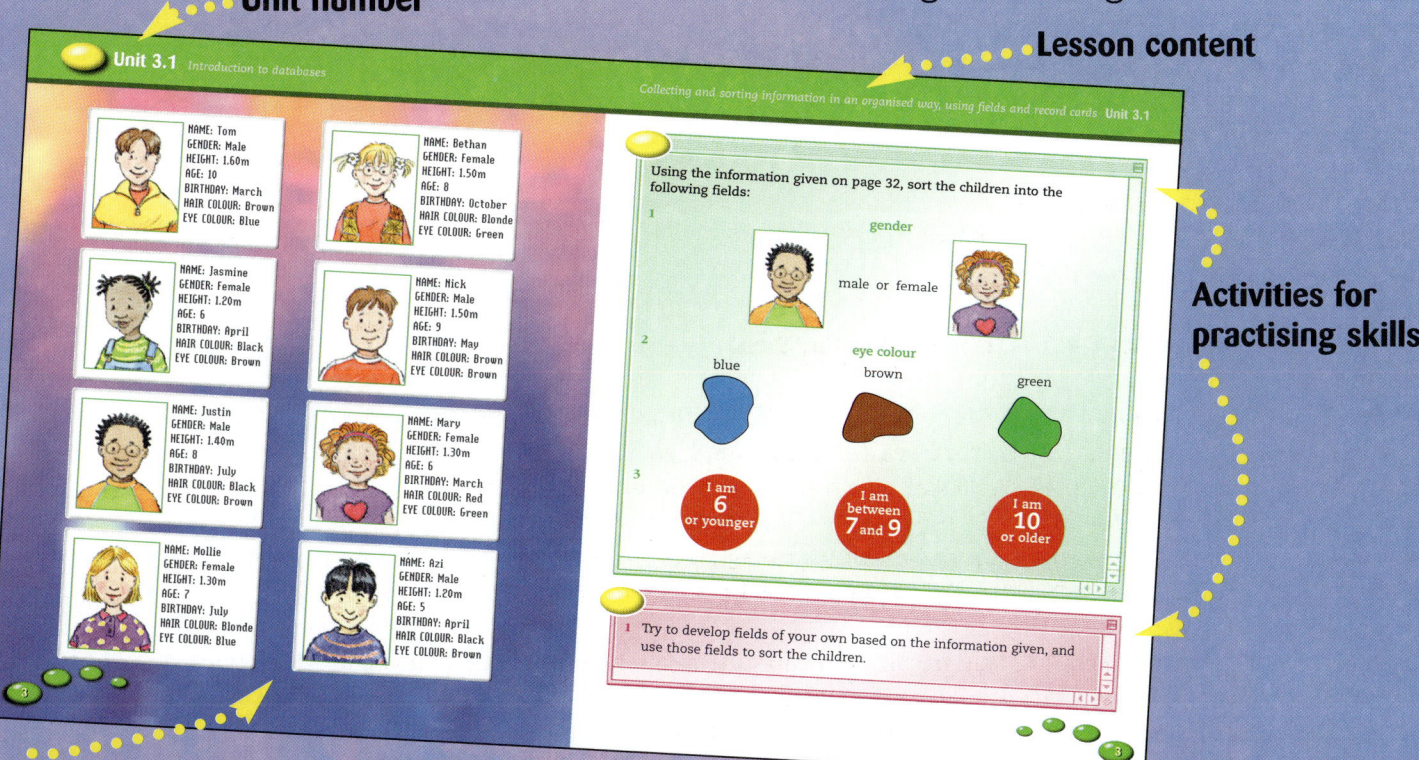

Unit number

Lesson content

Activities for practising skills

Text and pictures for reading and discussion

The Glossary

At the back of this book there is a glossary which contains and gives examples of key words. The explanations of key ICT vocabulary may be used for teaching purposes, or as a handy reference by the children.

Contents grid

PAGE NUMBER		LESSON TITLE	
8 – 9		1.1	Combining text and graphics
10 – 11		1.2	Combining text and graphics
12 – 13		1.3	Combining text and graphics
14 – 15		1.4	Combining text and graphics
16 – 17		1.5	Combining text and graphics
18 – 19		1.6	Combining text and graphics
20 – 21		1.7	Combining text and graphics
22 – 23		1	Combining text and graphics INTEGRATED TASK
24 – 25		2.1	Manipulating sound
26 – 27		2.2	Manipulating sound
28 – 29		2.3	Manipulating sound
30 – 31		2	Manipulating sound INTEGRATED TASK
32 – 33		3.1	Introduction to databases
34 – 35		3.2	Introduction to databases
36 – 37		3.3	Introduction to databases
38 – 39		3.4	Introduction to databases
40 – 41		3	Introduction to databases INTEGRATED TASK
42 – 43		4.1	Simulations
44 – 45		4.2	Simulations
46 – 47		4	Simulations INTEGRATED TASK
48 – 49		5.1	E-mails
50 – 51		5.2	E-mails
52 – 53		5	E-mails INTEGRATED TASK
54 – 64			Glossary and ICT Wordsearch

Contents grid

LESSON CONTENT	CURRICULUM LINK
Using font size and type to produce different effects	Literacy
Using font size, type and colour for advertisements	Literacy
Highlighting text, over typing and saving changes	Literacy
Inserting a graphic from a clip art file and resizing	Literacy
Copying and pasting graphics from a CD ROM	Literacy
Using the shift key to type upper case letters and characters such as question marks and speech marks	Literacy
Centre, left and right aligning	Literacy
Combine text and graphics to communicate information in the form of a magazine	Literacy
Recording sounds	Music
Using symbols to organise and reorganise sounds	Music
Combining electronic and live sounds	Music
Using ICT to create, organise and reorganise sounds	Music
Collecting and sorting information in an organised way using fields and record cards	Maths & Science
Exploring record cards stored as numbers	Maths & Science
Creating and searching databases	Maths & Science
Using database information to create bar charts	Maths & Science
Using a database and bar chart to sort, classify and present information	Maths & Cross curricular
Exploring options using a history CD ROM	History
Evaluating computer simulations	Cross curricular
Exploring the effects of changing variables in simulations	Cross curricular
Reading, annotating and replying to e-mails	Literacy
Using an address book and adding attachments	Literacy & Cross curricular
Gathering, exchanging and developing information using e-mail	Literacy & Cross curricular

The Computer

A printer prints out data onto paper in the form of text or graphics. There are different types of printers that have different ways of working. Black and white printers are more common, while colour printers are more expensive and often slower.

The monitor displays text (letters and numbers) and graphics (pictures) on a screen which looks a bit like a television screen. The screen may be colour, greyscale (showing different shades of grey) or monochrome (showing black with one other colour).

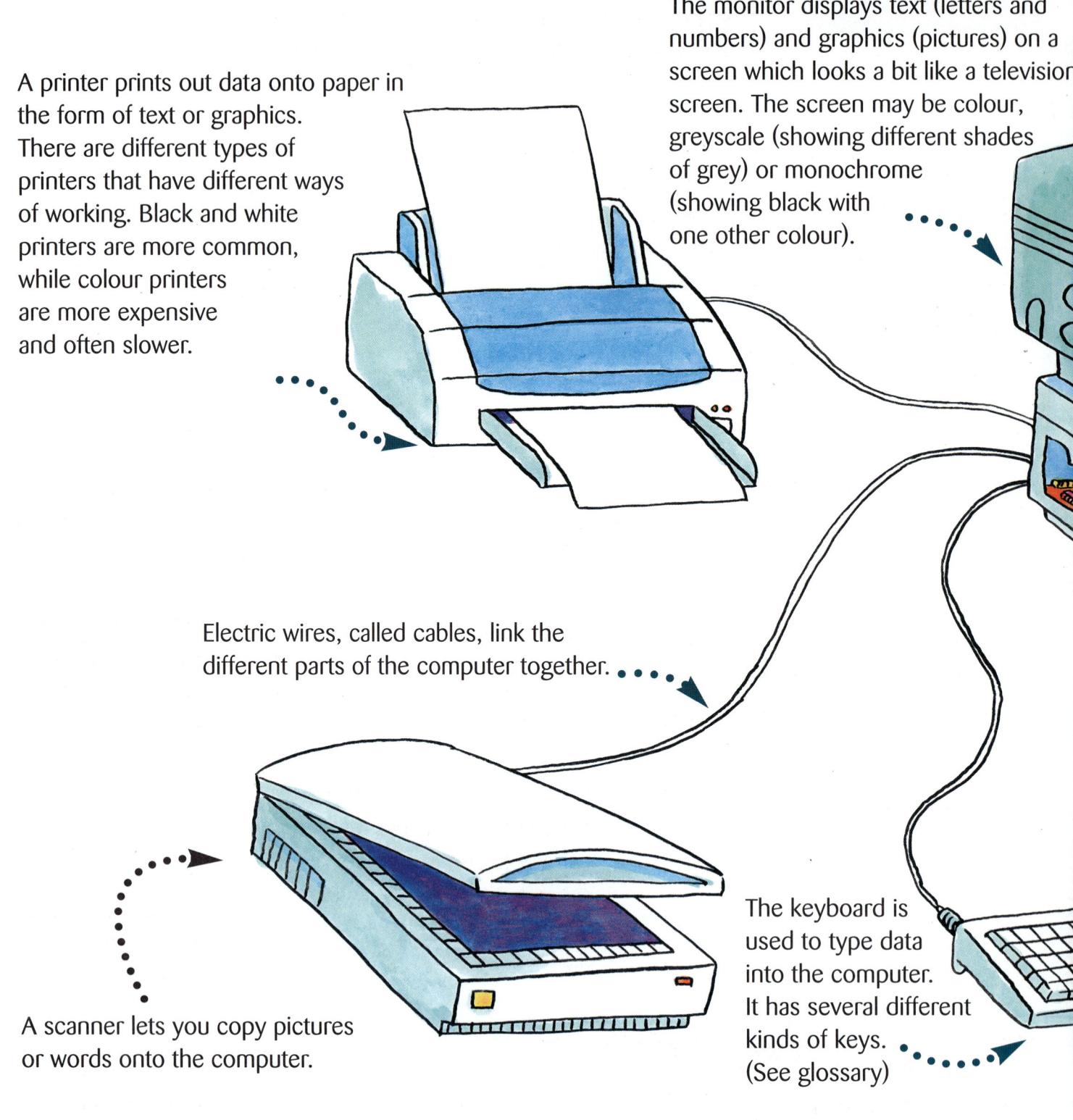

Electric wires, called cables, link the different parts of the computer together.

A scanner lets you copy pictures or words onto the computer.

The keyboard is used to type data into the computer. It has several different kinds of keys. (See glossary)

Multimedia means using computers to combine text, sound, graphics and video. Multimedia software usually comes on a CD ROM. To use multimedia you need to have a set of extra hardware called a multimedia bundle or kit, which includes a CD ROM drive.

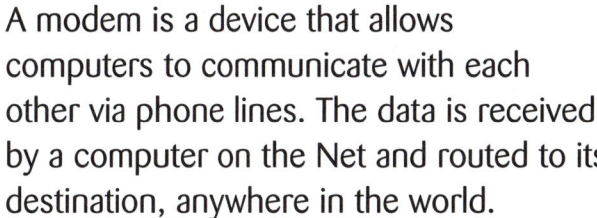

A modem is a device that allows computers to communicate with each other via phone lines. The data is received by a computer on the Net and routed to its destination, anywhere in the world.

Hard disks are the inside storage of the computer. They work in the same way as floppy disks but they are made of metal and can hold a lot more data. This is where most people keep all their software and files organised.

The disk drive holds disks. Some computers have more than one. A floppy disk fits into the computer's floppy disk drive. The drive spins the disk while a read/write head reads the data from it or writes new data onto it.

The mouse controls a pointer on the screen. You press the mouse buttons to select different choices. You select choices by clicking, double clicking or clicking and dragging.

The space the computer takes up on a desk or table top is called its footprint.

A mouse pad or mat is a rubbery mat with a smooth surface. The mouse works better on these than on a table top.

For further information see *The Usbourne Computer Dictionary*, Anna Claybourne and Mark Wallace, 1999.

Unit 1.1 Combining text and graphics

The Hiderhip

The Hiderhip is huge and hairy,
The Hiderhip is very scary.
It has long ears and sharp, sharp teeth,
Its nose is small with a moustache underneath.

The Hiderhip is big and tall,
So it lies in wait behind high walls.
Then it leaps right out on girls or boys
And gobbles them up with a crunching noise.

The Hiderhip is **HUGE** and hairy,

The Hiderhip is very SCARY.

It has long ears and SHARP, SHARP teeth,

Its nose is small with a moustache underneath.

Using font size and type to produce different effects **Unit 1.1**

1 Try changing some of these words to make them look more like their meaning.

| shout | rainbow | round | crash | fast |
| earthquake | stop | explosion | splash | bang |

2 Copy these sentences, making one word in each look like its meaning.
– Sam dropped the expensive vase and it smashed on the tiled floor.
– The hedgehog was very prickly.
– The mountaineers climbed up the very steep mountain.
– The feather tickled Dan's nose. 'Attishoo!' he sneezed.
– The door creaked open and the giant looked up slowly from his newspaper.
– The seagull dived into the icy water.

3 Write this poem out and change some of the words to look like their meaning.

Open door
Creaky floor
Peer around
Make no sound
Tiptoe and creep
Everyone's asleep
I'm a beast
Looking for a midnight feast!

# Unit 1.2 *Combining text and graphics*

Come and enjoy all the latest sounds…

Don't miss out – be around!

What: Disco

Where: School Hall

When: Friday night from 7 –10pm

Cost: £1.00

Flashing lights and tunes to hum,

Make a note of the date…

And make sure you come!

Using font size, type and colour for advertisements **Unit 1.2**

1. Design a poster using one of the texts below. Think about the audience and how you can make your poster more eye-catching. Change the style, size and colour of the text so it will grab people's attention.

   Come and see your children perform

   School concert

   Friday 11th December

   7pm

   Don't miss it!

   What: Bring and buy sale
   When: Saturday 20th October
   Doors open from 2pm
   Cost: Entrance 20p

   Cakes and refreshments
   Games and competitions
   Grand raffle
   Bargains galore!
   Face painting
   Toys
   Books
   Plants
   Clothes

   Fun for all the family.
   Come and check it out!

2. Make up your own poster to advertise your school's sports day or another school event. Plan the poster and sketch it out, ready to create on the computer. Think about:
   - font style
   - font colours
   - font sizes.

Unit 1.3 Combining text and graphics

There's a ghost in my bag

Mrs Shah was at the front of the class explaining how to do multiplication on the board.

Out of the corner of his eye, Tom saw a slight movement in his bag. He nudged Sarah.

'Look,' he said quietly in her ear.

'What's the matter?' Sarah said.

'My bag is moving,' Tom said.

Mrs Shah noticed that Tom and Sarah were not paying attention. She looked at them crossly.

'What are you two doing?' she said.

Tom said, 'There's a ghost in my bag!'

'Don't be so silly!' Mrs Shah said, as she came over to see for herself.

Tom leaned over and slowly opened the top of his bag.

'Help!' he said, as he leapt from his chair. 'There's a rat in my bag!'

Sarah smiled. 'Don't panic! It's just the class hamster!' she said.

'Well, what's it doing in Tom's bag?' Mrs Shah said.

'I expect it's looking for something to eat,' Sarah said.

At this, the whole class roared with laughter.

'I think you'd better put it back in its cage, Sarah, so we can get on,' said Mrs Shah.

Highlighting text, over typing and saving changes **Unit 1.3**

1. Create your own word bank of words to use instead of *said*. Start with those that you have already collected as a class.

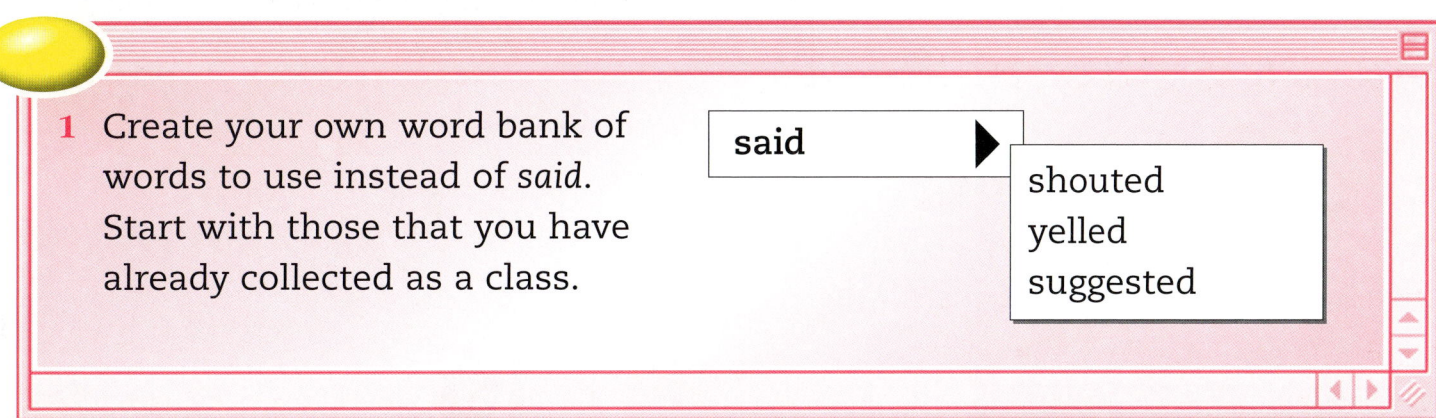

2. Copy out these sentences and use the best words from your list to replace the word *said* in each one.
   - 'Who broke the window?' the man *said* angrily.
   - 'Tiptoe quietly, or you will wake the baby,' Mrs Jones *said*.
   - 'Look out!' Charlie *said*, as the car veered towards them on the pavement.
   - 'It's just so unfair!' Liz *said* under her breath.
   - 'You have to turn right after these traffic lights and then take the first left,' the police officer *said*.
   - 'Please don't eat me!' Joe *said* to the dragon.

3. Write some speech sentences of your own. Use the word *said* in all of them. Swap sentences with a partner and try to make each other's texts sound more interesting.

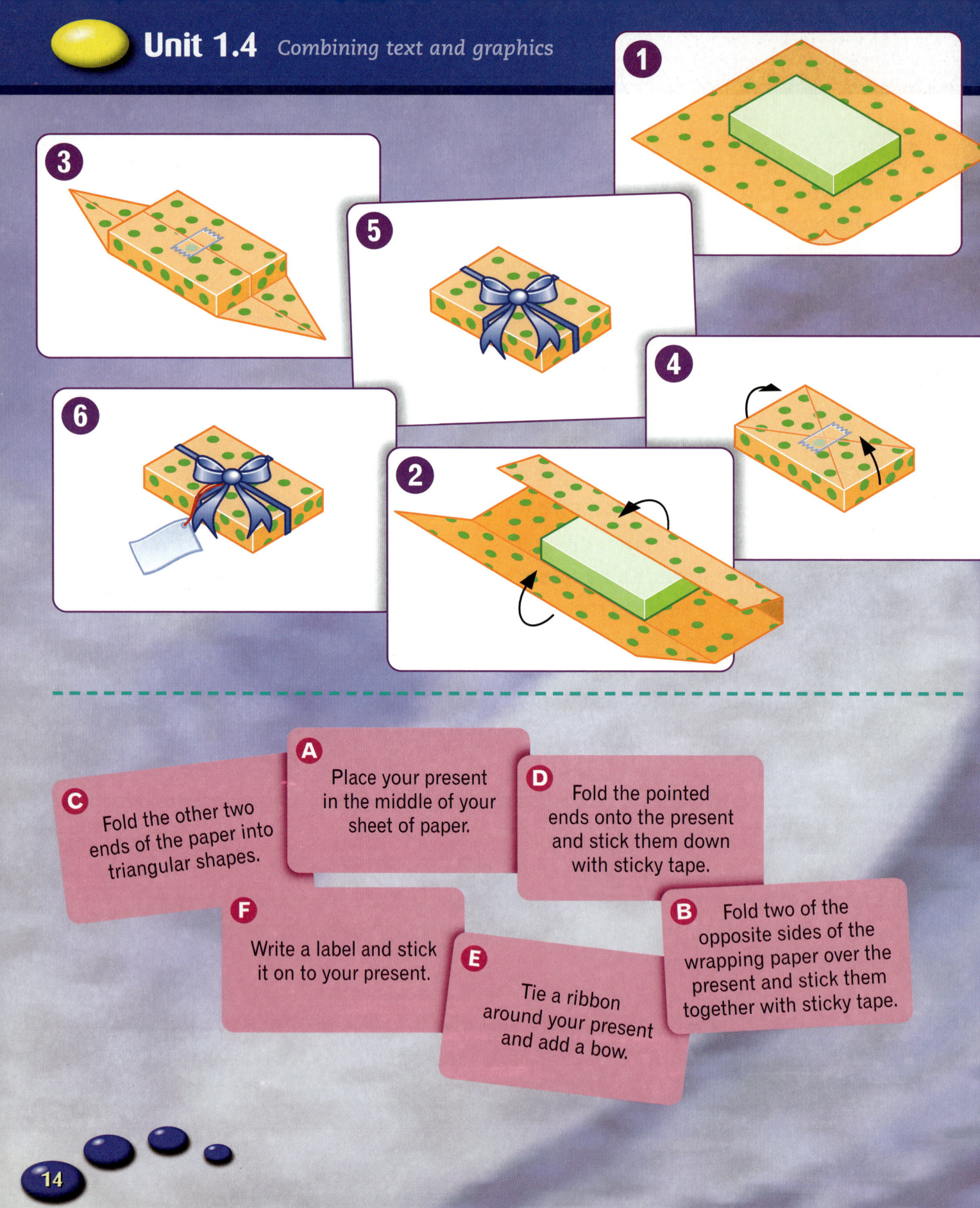

Inserting a graphic from a clip art file and resizing **Unit 1.4**

A Find a safe place to cross the road, not near parked cars.

B Stop a little way back from the edge of the kerb.

C Look in every direction.

D Listen carefully for any traffic.

E When it is safe, walk straight across the road. Always walk, never run.

F Keep looking and listening all the time while you cross.

 **Unit 1.5** Combining text and graphics

WONDERS of the ANCIENT WORLD

The pyramids of Giza in Egypt were the tombs of ancient Egyptian kings and queens. They were buried with everything they thought they might need in their next life, such as jewels, food and furniture.

King Mausolus built the grandest tomb in the world, at Halicarnassus in Turkey. A new word was invented after Mausolus to describe the tomb – mausoleum.

The beautiful Hanging Gardens of Babylon were built by King Nebuchadnezzar for his wife. They were filled with colourful plants and grand structures shaped like pyramids.

Copying and pasting graphics from a CD ROM **Unit 1.5**

1. Match these pictures to the correct text.

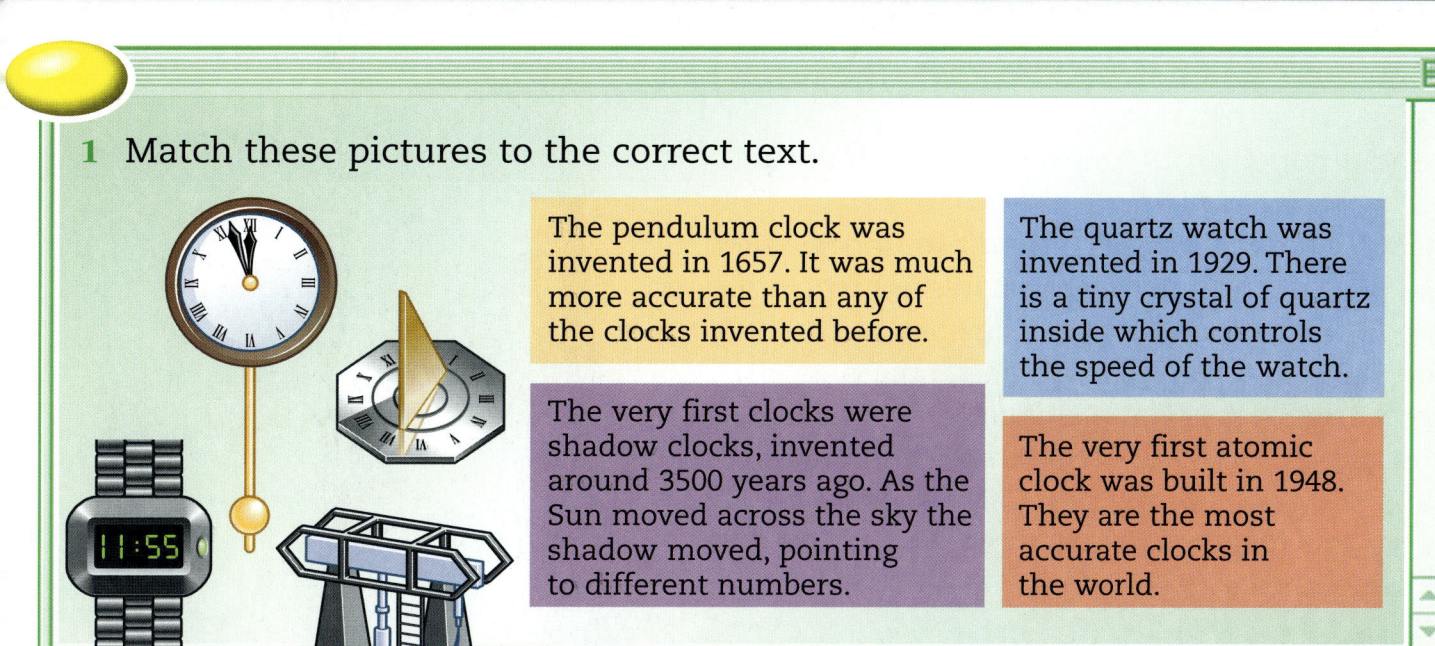

The pendulum clock was invented in 1657. It was much more accurate than any of the clocks invented before.

The quartz watch was invented in 1929. There is a tiny crystal of quartz inside which controls the speed of the watch.

The very first clocks were shadow clocks, invented around 3500 years ago. As the Sun moved across the sky the shadow moved, pointing to different numbers.

The very first atomic clock was built in 1948. They are the most accurate clocks in the world.

2. Find out about these four methods of transport. Copy out the pictures and write some sentences to go with each one.

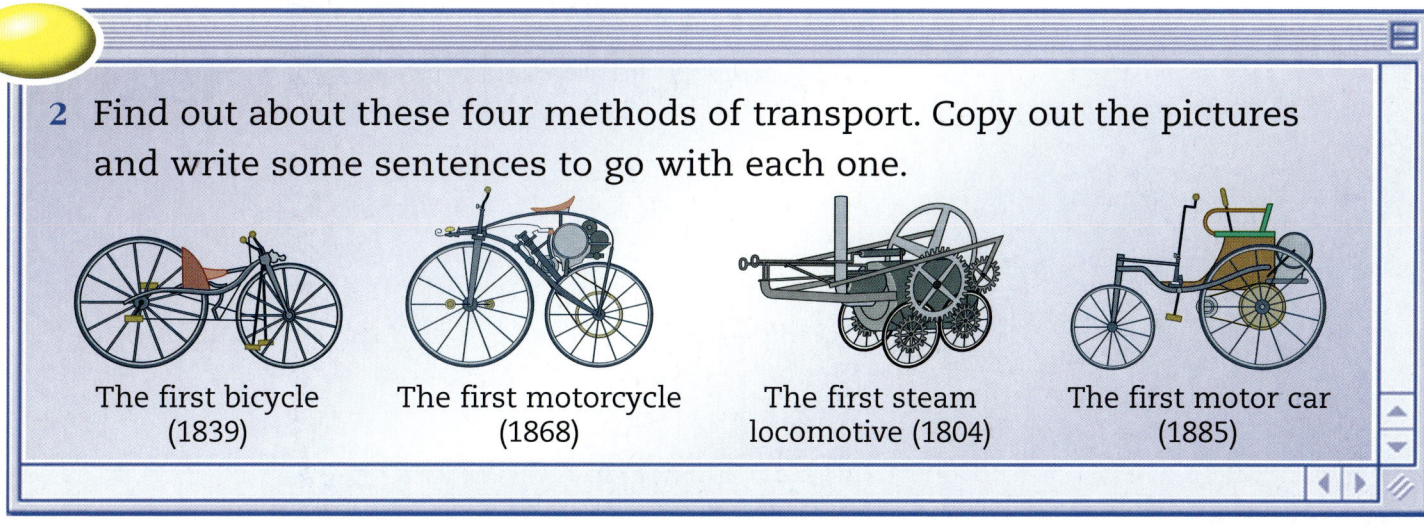

The first bicycle (1839)

The first motorcycle (1868)

The first steam locomotive (1804)

The first motor car (1885)

3. Find out some information about a history topic of your choice, using reference books or the Internet. Copy or print out four pictures for your chosen topic and write some sentences to go with them.

Unit 1.6 Combining text and graphics

mr and mrs jones stopped outside the restaurant. it was called the hungry horse.
are you hungry mrs jones asked her husband.
yes, i am, he replied.
shall we have lunch here then mrs jones asked.
yes, it looks fine mr jones answered. they opened the door and went inside. they sat at the only free table by a roaring fire and looked at the menu together. what are you going to have mr jones asked his wife. i think i'll have fish and chips she replied, and you? i think i'm going to try the frog soup! just then the waitress arrived to take their order.

Mr and Mrs Jones stopped outside the restaurant. It was called the Hungry Horse. 'Are you hungry?' Mrs Jones asked her husband.
'Yes, I am,' he replied.
'Shall we have lunch here, then?' Mrs Jones asked.
'Yes, it looks fine,' Mr Jones answered.

they opened the door and went inside. they sat at the only free table by a roaring fire and looked at the menu together. what are you going to have mr jones asked his wife.
i think i'll have fish and chips she replied, and you?
i think i'm going to try the frog soup!
just then the waitress arrived to take their order.

Using the shift key to type upper case letters and characters **Unit 1.6**

1. Rewrite these sentences correctly, putting in all the missing capital letters.
   - aunt jean's birthday is in june.
   - france, germany and italy are all countries in europe.
   - last august i stayed at the grand hotel in brighton.
   - mr and mrs chan went to see a film at the odeon on wednesday night.

2. Copy these sentences. Punctuate each question correctly and write a suitable answer for each one.
   - what colour is a banana
   - do you have a pet
   - when is your birthday and how old will you be this year
   - what makes you happy

3. Copy these sentences and punctuate them correctly. Put in the missing capital letters, speech marks and question marks.
   - why are you walking on my lawn mr steel shouted.
   - i'm walking because i can't fly! sean answered.
   - the mechanic at the busy bee garage said there's a problem with your brakes. mrs shelly asked can you fix them by saturday.
   - pete's mum said you can have fish fingers or beefburgers for tea. which do you want pete replied fish fingers are my favourite, i'd like those.
   - dr aziz asked what seems to be the problem mrs riddle replied my back is really painful just here.

Unit 1.7 Combining text and graphics

You are invited to Emil's birthday party

On: Saturday 5th May

At: 12 Young Street, Cambridge, CB1 2LZ

Time: 2pm–5pm

RSVP

You are invited to
EMIL'S BIRTHDAY PARTY

ON Saturday 5th May
AT 12 Young Street, Cambridge, CB1 2LZ
TIME 2pm–5pm

RSVP

1 Choose one of the texts below to design as an invitation. Arrange the information to make the invitation interesting and easy to read. Think about the size of the text and how it should be aligned.

You are invited to Karen and Joel's summer pool party
At: the Leisureside centre in Cardiff
On: Friday 15th August
From: 6–9pm
Don't forget to bring your costume and a towel

Barbie's Birthday Barbecue
At: Perranporth Beach
On: 22nd May
From: 2pm–'til dark
Beach games and swimming included
rsvp

2 Make up your own information and design an invitation for one of these events:
- A birthday party
- A school event
- A wedding
- A sporting event
- The opening of a new restaurant or cinema
- An exhibition.

Add some hand-drawn pictures to make your invitation more attractive and appealing.

Unit 1 Combining text and graphics INTEGRATED TASK

Look at the selection of magazine pages below.

Combine text and graphics to communicate information in the form of a class magazine **Unit 1**

You are going to produce a class magazine.
You will need to decide with your teacher which page in the magazine your group is going to make.

Use the examples on page 22 to help you decide what your page will be about and how it will look. You will need to write the text and do a rough design before you go to the computer.

When you are making your page remember to use some of the skills you have learnt in this unit. Use this checklist as a handy reminder:

- [ ] Using different font sizes and different types of font
- [ ] Choosing different font colours
- [ ] Highlighting and replacing words
- [ ] Choosing graphics from clip art files, stored on the computer (and your own pictures that have been saved)
- [ ] Selecting graphics from CD ROMs
- [ ] Using the shift keys when using capital letters, speech marks and question marks
- [ ] Centring, left aligning and right aligning text to create interesting and eye-catching layouts.

Try to remember any problems you have when making your page and any ways you think using the computer made it easier. You can share these with the class when your magazine is finished.

Unit 2.1 *Manipulating sound*

Talk about the instruments in the picture below and how they make a sound.

Recording sounds **Unit 2.1**

1 Talk about the pictures of the instruments below.

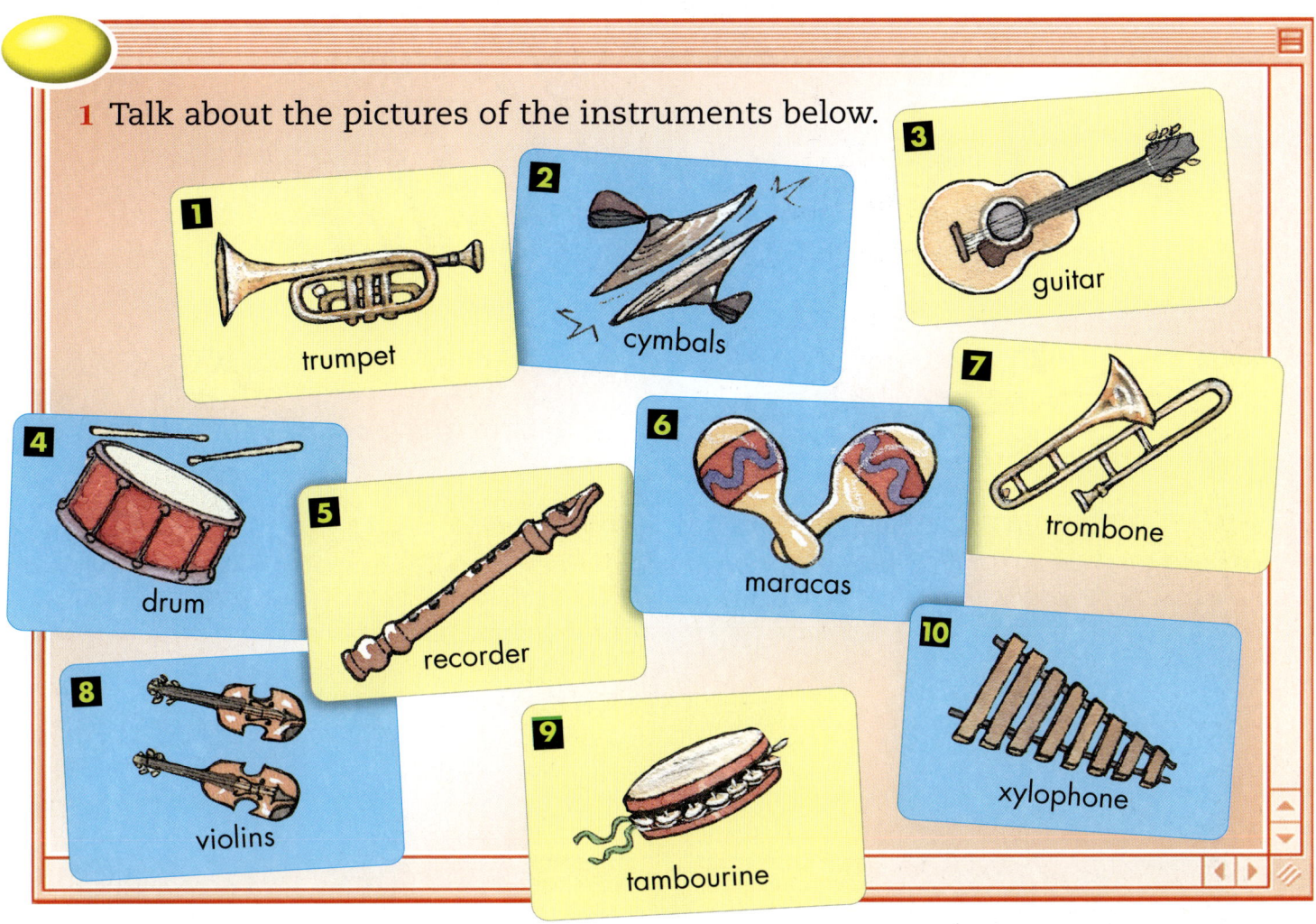

2 Can you put the instruments above into their instrument families? Copy this chart. Write the instrument names in the correct columns.

Wind	String	Percussion
Recorder		

3 Write two more instruments of your own in each column of the chart.

Unit 2.2 *Manipulating sound*

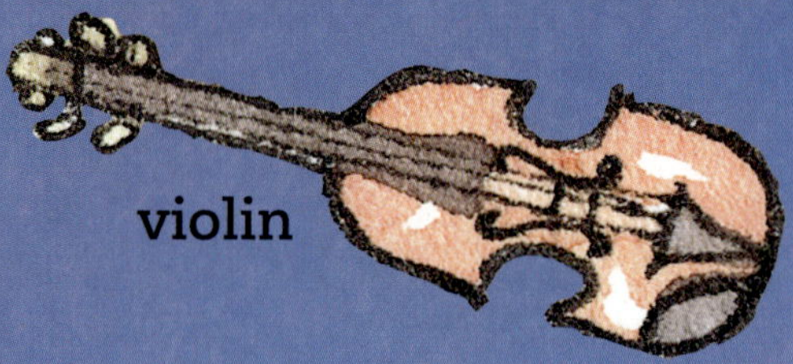

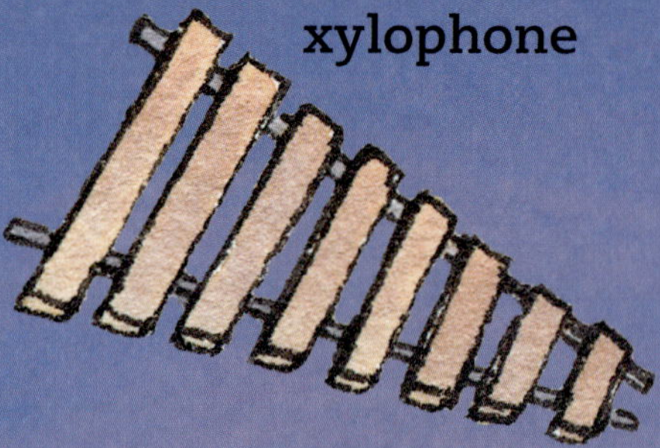

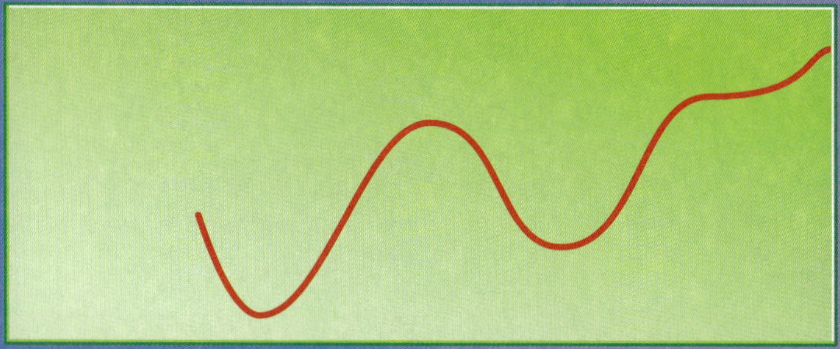

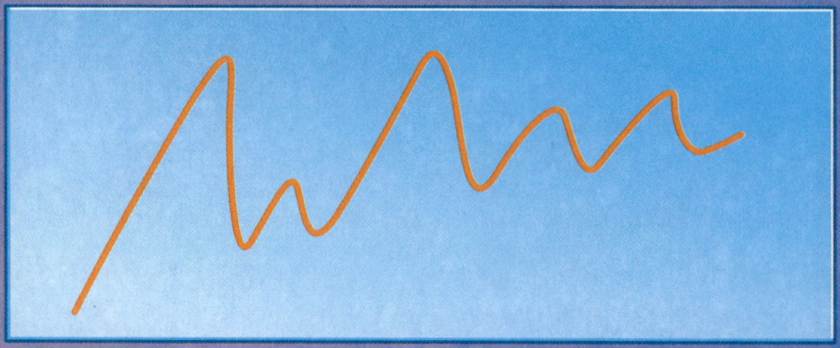

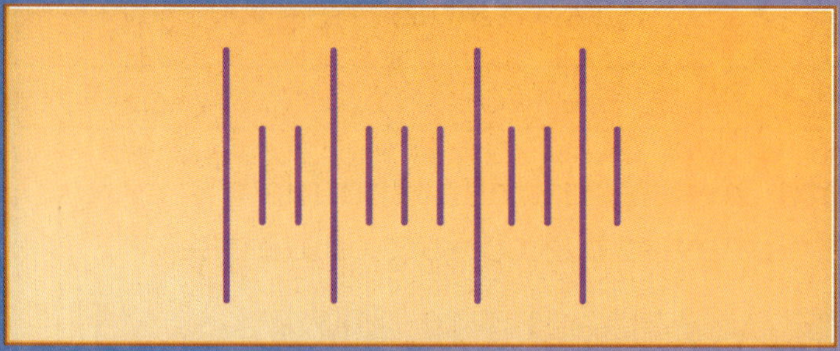

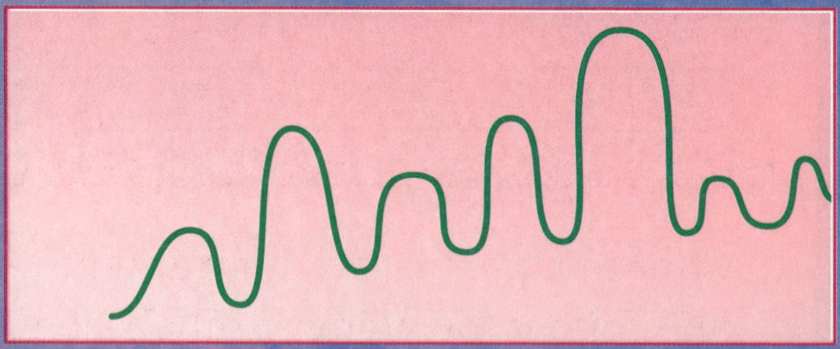

Can you match the instruments above to the correct symbol card?

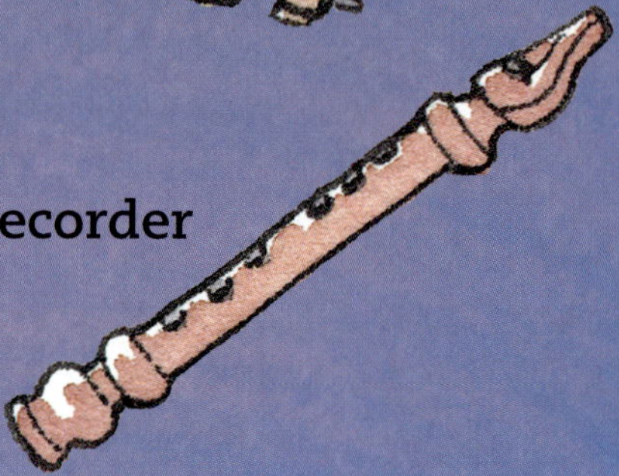

Using symbols to organise and reorganise sounds Unit 2.2

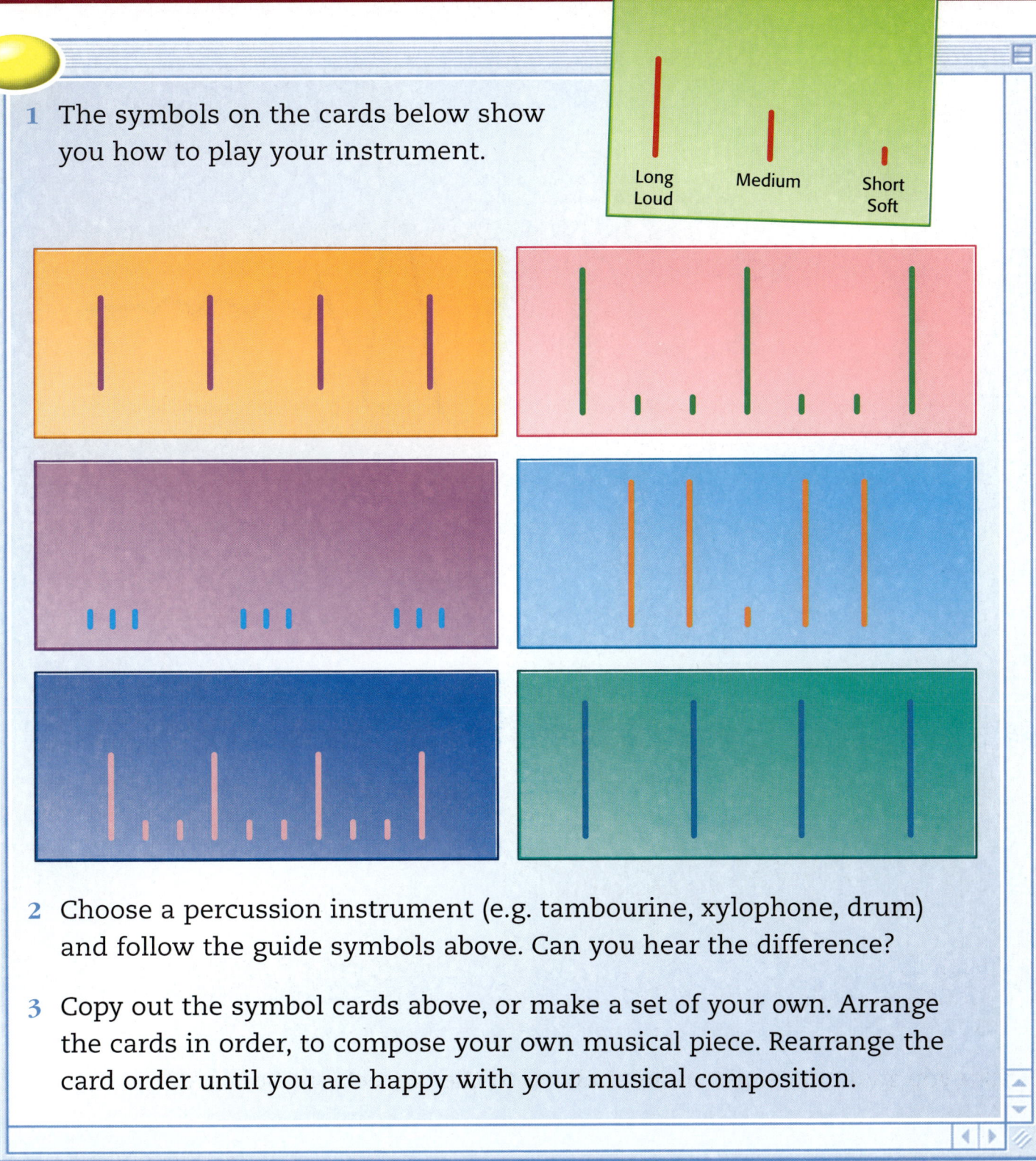

1 The symbols on the cards below show you how to play your instrument.

2 Choose a percussion instrument (e.g. tambourine, xylophone, drum) and follow the guide symbols above. Can you hear the difference?

3 Copy out the symbol cards above, or make a set of your own. Arrange the cards in order, to compose your own musical piece. Rearrange the card order until you are happy with your musical composition.

Unit 2.3 *Manipulating sound*

Talk about these symbol cards.

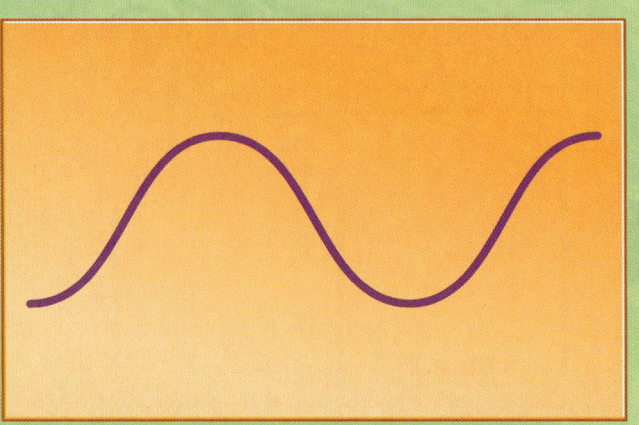

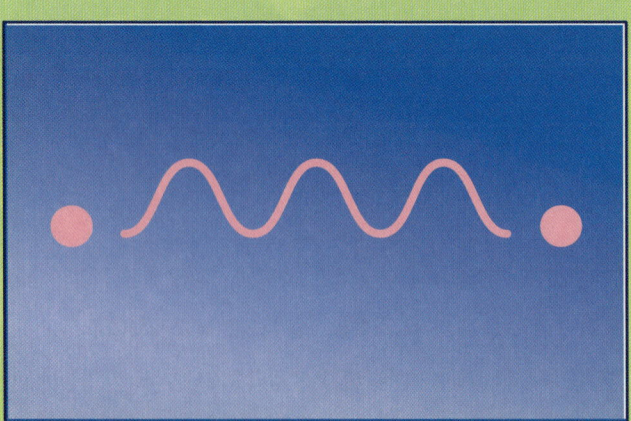
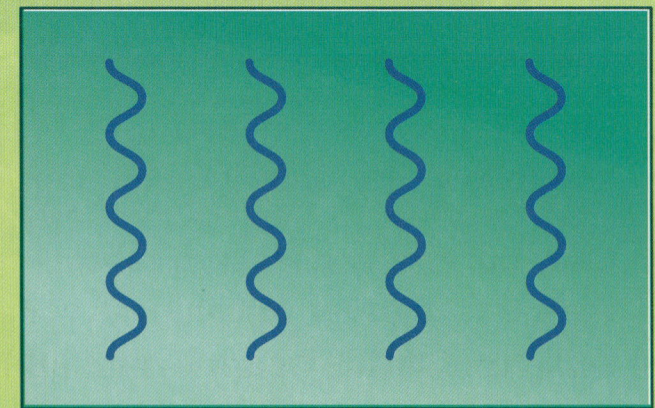

Combining electronic and live sounds **Unit 2.3**

1. Use the symbol cards below to help you create a 'loop' (repeated section of music).

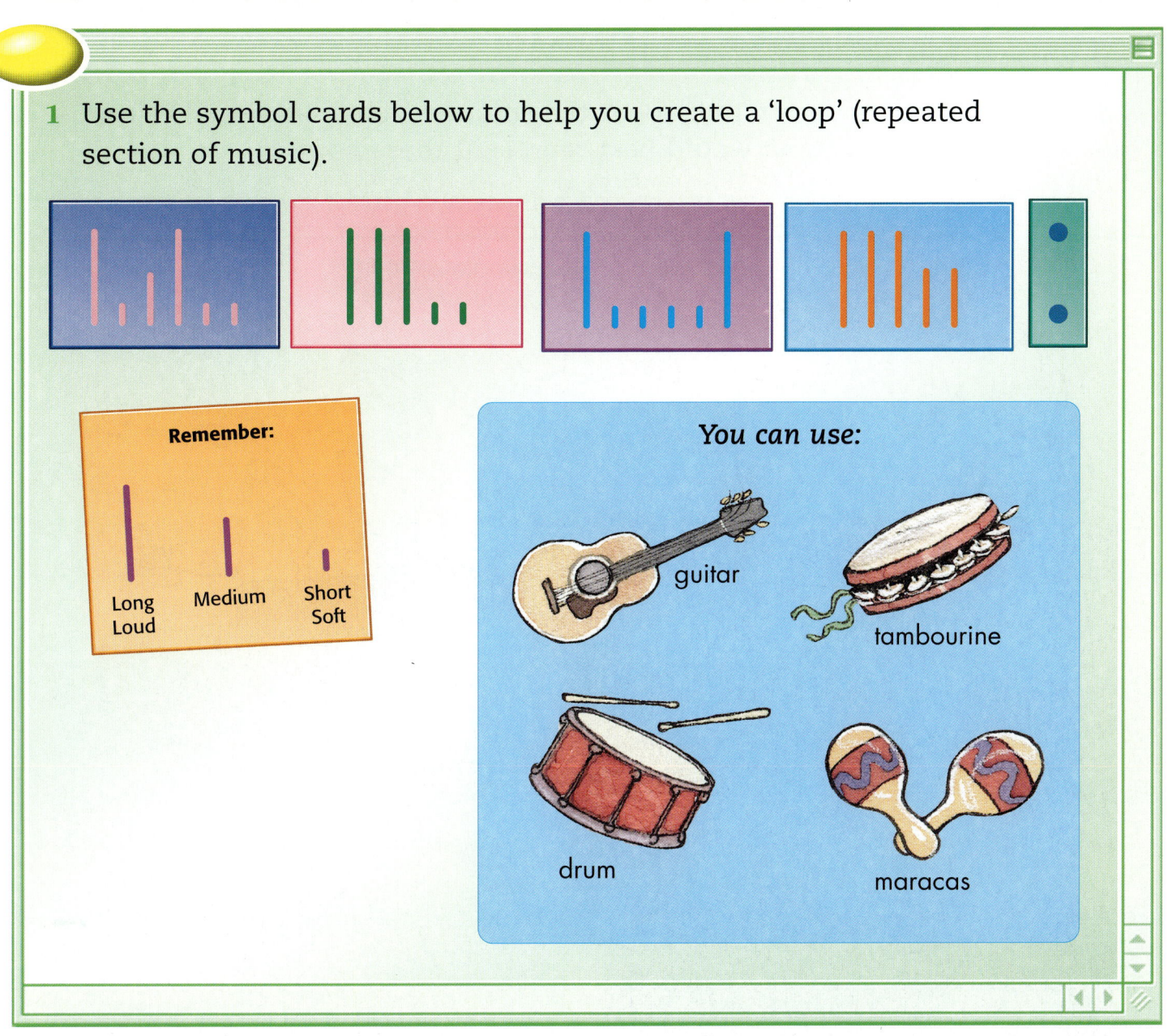

2. Make your own set of symbol cards. Use them to create your own loop. Swap cards with a partner and perform each other's compositions.

Unit 2 *Manipulating sound* INTEGRATED TASK

Look at the pictures below. Talk about the sounds each animal makes and the instruments you think would best represent these sounds.

Elephant

Kangaroo

Monkeys

Fish

Snake

Lion

Using ICT to create, organise and reorganise sounds Unit 2

You are going to compose a piece of music to represent an animal. Working in small groups, choose one of the animals opposite or think of one of your own.

Think about the kind of music and sounds you need to represent your animal. Have a good idea about this before you use the computer. Decide, also, which live instruments you will use to go with your computer composed piece.

Make notes about these things so you can make the most of your time at the computer. You can use some of the symbol recording ideas to help you compose a live instrument beat to go with your final piece.

You will need to use the skills that you have learnt in this unit:

- [ ] ICT in the form of a tape recorder can be used to record sounds
- [ ] A CD ROM is like this, but it tends to sound a lot better!
- [ ] Icons on the computer (small computer symbols) show a small musical phrase that can be put together in a group to create a musical piece
- [ ] Live music can be recorded to place with a computer composed piece
- [ ] Symbols can be drawn and recorded on paper for live instrument work that are like the icons on the computer compose program.

When you have completed your piece, or while you are waiting for your turn at the computer, draw a picture of your animal which the rest of the class will try and match to your piece of music.

You might like to show your animal hunting, eating, with its young or resting – think of the best way to illustrate your animal to help the rest of the class see the type of animal it is and how your music is reflecting its nature.

Unit 3.1 Introduction to databases

NAME: Tom
GENDER: Male
HEIGHT: 1.60m
AGE: 10
BIRTHDAY: March
HAIR COLOUR: Brown
EYE COLOUR: Blue

NAME: Bethan
GENDER: Female
HEIGHT: 1.50m
AGE: 8
BIRTHDAY: October
HAIR COLOUR: Blonde
EYE COLOUR: Green

NAME: Jasmine
GENDER: Female
HEIGHT: 1.20m
AGE: 6
BIRTHDAY: April
HAIR COLOUR: Black
EYE COLOUR: Brown

NAME: Nick
GENDER: Male
HEIGHT: 1.50m
AGE: 9
BIRTHDAY: May
HAIR COLOUR: Brown
EYE COLOUR: Brown

NAME: Justin
GENDER: Male
HEIGHT: 1.40m
AGE: 8
BIRTHDAY: July
HAIR COLOUR: Black
EYE COLOUR: Brown

NAME: Mary
GENDER: Female
HEIGHT: 1.30m
AGE: 6
BIRTHDAY: March
HAIR COLOUR: Red
EYE COLOUR: Green

NAME: Mollie
GENDER: Female
HEIGHT: 1.30m
AGE: 7
BIRTHDAY: July
HAIR COLOUR: Blonde
EYE COLOUR: Blue

NAME: Azi
GENDER: Male
HEIGHT: 1.20m
AGE: 5
BIRTHDAY: April
HAIR COLOUR: Black
EYE COLOUR: Brown

Collecting and sorting information in an organised way, using fields and record cards **Unit 3.1**

Using the information given on page 32, sort the children into the following fields:

1 **gender**

male or female

2 **eye colour**

blue   brown 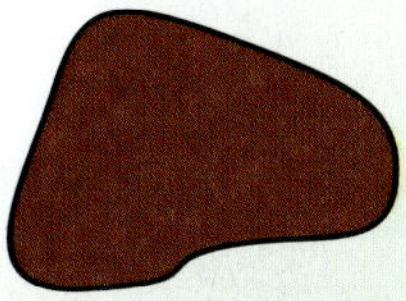   green

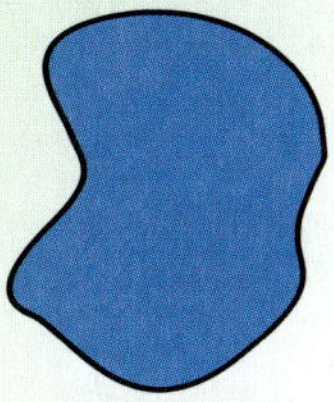

3

I am 6 or younger

I am between 7 and 9

I am 10 or older

1 Try to develop fields of your own based on the information given, and use those fields to sort the children.

Unit 3.2 Introduction to databases

1

name: grass snake
habitat: grassland
colour: green
number of legs: 0
wings: no
food: birds, small mammals

2

name: goldfish
habitat: fresh water
colour: orange/red
number of legs: 0
wings: no
food: plants, insects and worms

3

name: frog
habitat: land and water
colour: green/brown
number of legs: 4
wings: no
food: insects and worms

4

name: camel
habitat: desert
colour: brown
number of legs: 4
wings: no
food: plants

5

name: ostrich
habitat: African grassland
colour: brown/grey
number of legs: 2
wings: yes, but flightless
food: plants and small reptiles

6

name: bat
habitat: caves/lofts/trees
colour: black/brown
number of legs: 4
wings: yes
food: fruit and insects

7

name: domestic pig
habitat: farmland
colour: pink
number of legs: 4
wings: no
food: plants

8

name: penguins
habitat: Antarctic waters
colour: black and white
number of legs: 2
wings: yes, but flightless
food: fish

Exploring record cards stored as numbers **Unit 3.2**

1. Copy and complete this chart, using the record cards on page 34.

Green animals	Animals with no legs	Animals that eat plants	Animals with wings

2. Find and list the record cards that have:
   - animals with four legs
   - animals that live in water and eat plants and insects
   - animals that have no legs and eat other animals.

3. Make four more record cards of your own to add to the file, using the same fields.

```
name:
habitat:
colour:
number of legs:
wings:
food:
```

Unit 3.3 Introduction to databases

Hedgehogs are brown and have four legs. They live on land in dark, sheltered places. They do not have wings. They use their sense of smell to find insects, snails, grubs and frogs to eat.

Snails can live on land and in water. They have no wings and only one large muscular 'foot'. Their shells are usually patterned brown and they live in gardens or ponds where there is plenty of rotting plant material for them to eat.

Chimpanzees live in the forests of central and western Africa where they eat mainly leaves and fruit. They are black/brown in colour and have four legs but no wings.

Octopuses live in shallow sea water, hiding in rocky dens. They have eight legs which they use to catch other sea creatures for food. They are a speckled brown colour and have no wings.

Grey seals spend most of their lives in the water, although they breathe air. They have two front legs and a strong tail for swimming, but no wings. They are grey and white in colour and hunt fish and shellfish to eat.

Macaws are brightly coloured in reds, greens and blues. They live in rainforests where they eat mainly fruit and nuts. They have two wings and two legs.

NAME:
HABITAT:
COLOUR:
NUMBER OF LEGS:
WINGS:
FOOD:

Creating and searching databases Unit 3.3

1. Choose one animal description from page 36 and make a record card from the information given. Use the blank card at the bottom of the page to help you.

2. Copy and complete these record cards, using the animal descriptions on page 36.

NAME: hedgehog
HABITAT:
COLOUR:
NUMBER OF LEGS: 4
WINGS:
FOOD:

NAME:
HABITAT: land and water
COLOUR:
NUMBER OF LEGS:
WINGS:
FOOD:

NAME:
HABITAT:
COLOUR: brightly coloured, red, green, blue
NUMBER OF LEGS:
WINGS: yes
FOOD:

NAME:
HABITAT: forests of central and western Africa
COLOUR:
NUMBER OF LEGS: 4
WINGS:
FOOD:

3. Create your own record cards for six animals of your choice. Use information books and other resources to find the information you need.

37

Unit 3.4 Introduction to databases

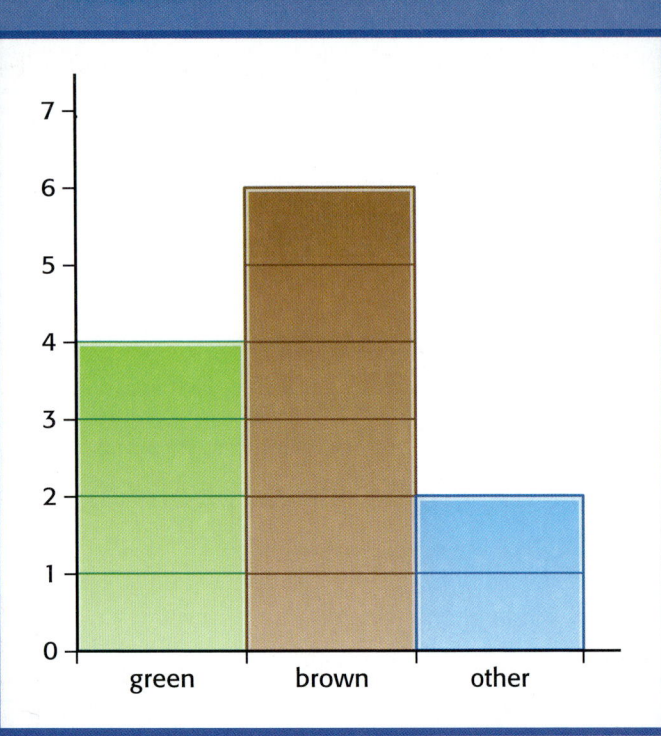

10
name: frog
habitat:
colour:
number of legs:
wings:
food:

5
name: lizard
habitat:
colour:
number of legs:
wings:
food:

2
name: snake
habitat:
colour:
number of legs:
wings:
food:

7
name: crocodile
habitat:
colour:
number of legs:
wings:
food:

3
name: zebra
habitat:
colour:
number of legs:
wings:
food:

4
name: bear
habitat:
colour:
number of legs:
wings:
food:

8
name: tropical fish
habitat:
colour:
number of legs:
wings:
food:

11
name: camel
habitat:
colour:
number of legs:
wings:
food:

6
name: monkey
habitat:
colour:
number of legs:
wings:
food:

1
name: dog
habitat:
colour:
number of legs:
wings:
food:

12
name: bird
habitat:
colour:
number of legs:
wings:
food:

9
name: tortoise
habitat:
colour:
number of legs:
wings:
food:

1. Ben has sorted his data cards into the field of *food*. Look at the bar chart he has drawn and talk about the information it shows.

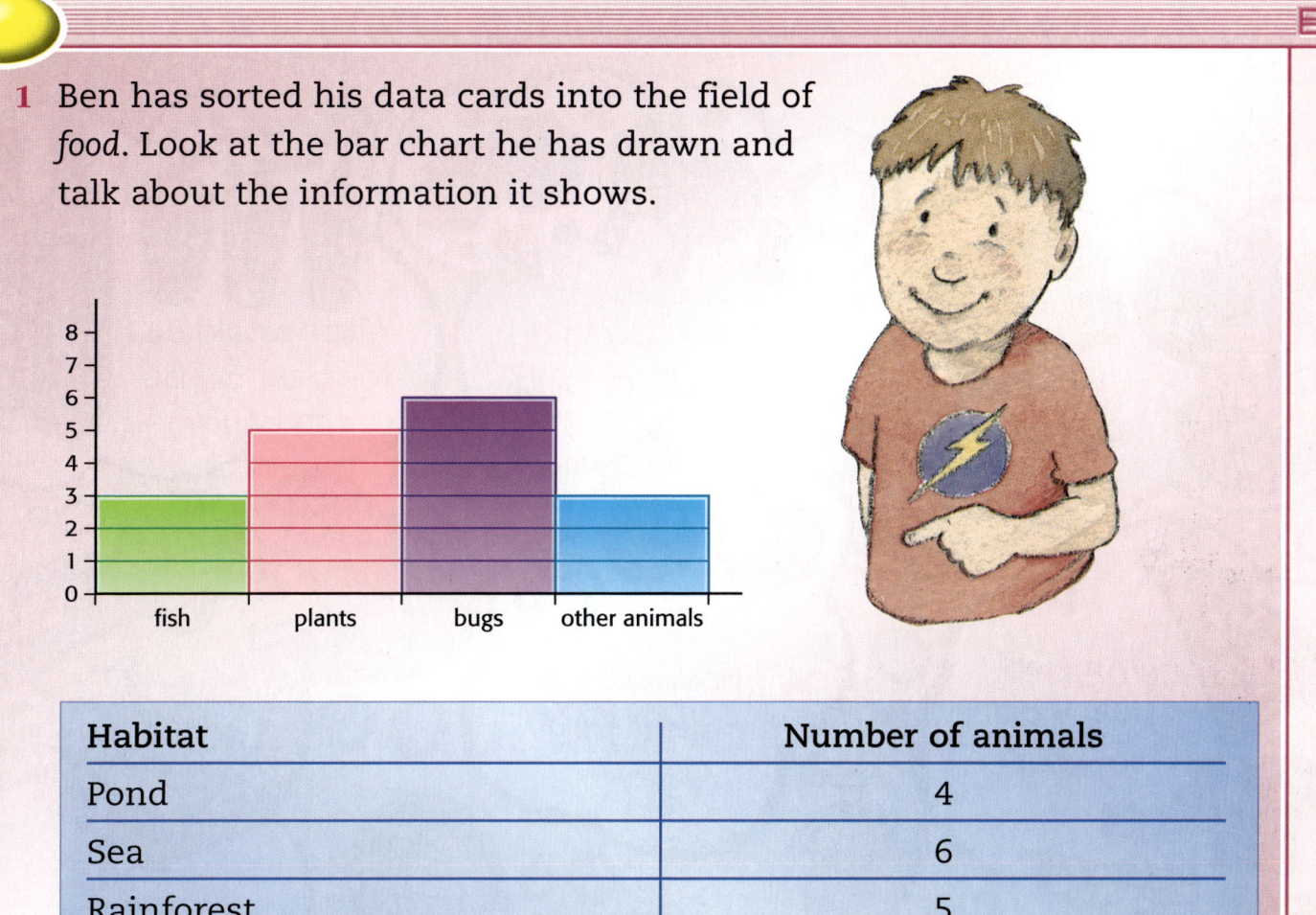

Habitat	Number of animals
Pond	4
Sea	6
Rainforest	5
Desert	2

3. Use the record cards that you set up as a class in Unit 3.3, question 3, to create a bar chart. Choose one field from the cards.

Unit 3 Introduction to databases INTEGRATED TASK

Anwar and Bethan want to organise a party for their class, but they don't know what everyone likes.

- What food will they want to eat?
- Which games do they like playing?
- What would be the best drinks to buy?
- What will they want to wear?
- How will we make it fair?
- What sort of music will everyone enjoy?

Using a database and bar chart to sort, classify and present information — Unit 3

You are going to plan your own class party but before you begin, you need to know what you will need to provide. Does everyone like the same food? Does everyone like listening and dancing to the same music?

By creating a database of everyone's likes and dislikes, you can find out what you will need to do to make the best party for everyone.

You will need to use the skills you have learnt in Unit 3:

- [ ] Information can be stored on record cards, in fields, e.g. hair colour
- [ ] Each record card has a number which you can use when you are searching through the file of cards
- [ ] You can find the answers to questions using a computer database, e.g. Which animals eat fish?
- [ ] You can make your own data/record cards to add to a database
- [ ] You can make a bar chart to *show* the answer to your question.

You will need to design data cards, to record the information you need on the class's likes and dislikes. When your group has filled in their data cards, enter this information into your class database. When everyone has entered their information your class teacher will tell you what area of the party you need to find out information for. You will need to turn this question into a way of searching the database.

When you have your information, print it out as a bar chart. You can share this information with your class in order to help organise the party. This will hopefully mean your party is fair!

Remember to think about how the computer helped you to do your job.

Unit 4.1 Simulations

Look at the activities below. Divide the activities into two groups: those you could do today and those you could not.

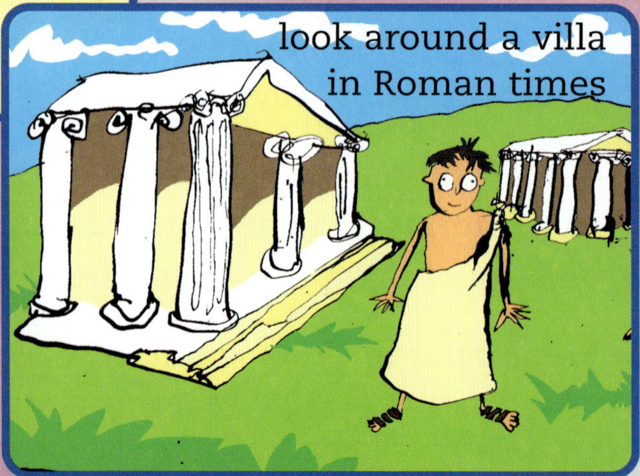

- drive a car
- play a game of football
- fly an aeroplane
- explore a city in another country
- go around the supermarket
- build a house
- look around a villa in Roman times

Exploring options using a history CD ROM **Unit 4.1**

Use information books about your current history topic to find answers to the questions below. You can use drawings to help with your answers.

What type of clothes did people wear?

_____

What did people eat?

_____

What did their houses look like?

_____

What types of jobs did people do?

_____

What were the schools like?

_____

What forms of transport were used?

_____

Unit 4.2 Simulations

Sean wants to know what it would be like to be an astronaut and travel in space. He has been using a computer simulation program.

Look at the questions he has been thinking about:

- Is it realistic?
- How is a simulation like, or not like, real life?
- Has any information been left out?
- How has it helped me understand more about being in space?

Evaluating computer simulations Unit 4.2

Use a computer simulation program at home or school.
Write a review about the program, using the framework below.

Name: _____

Date: _____

Computer simulation used: _____
_____

What was your computer simulation program about?
_____

Was it about a real or imaginary situation?
_____

Did you enjoy using it?
_____

Which part did you like best?
_____

What decisions did you have to make?
_____

Was there anything you couldn't do with it?
_____

How would you make the program better?
_____

What would be your top three activities to try on a simulation program?
_____

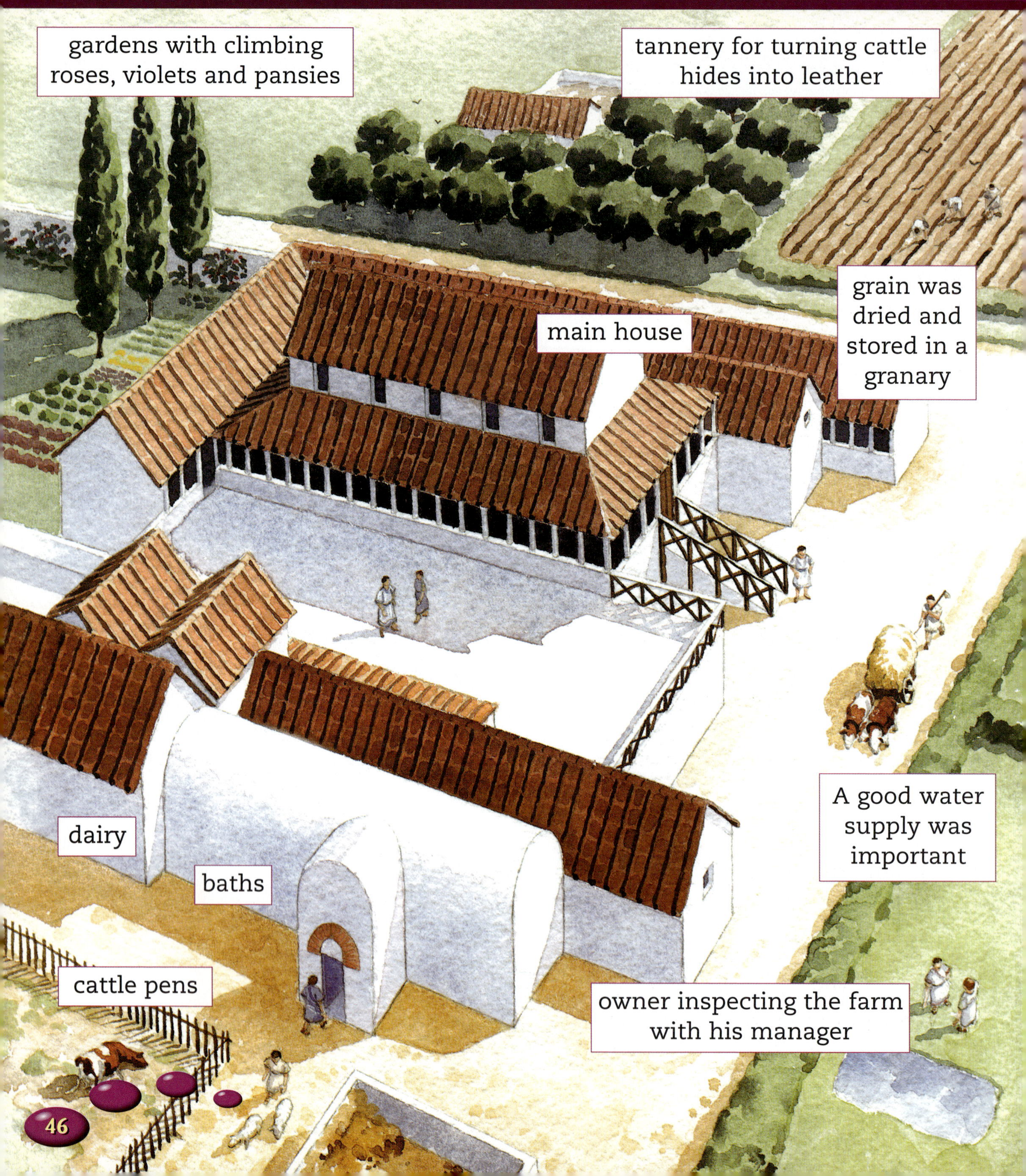

Unit 4 Simulations — INTEGRATED TASK

- gardens with climbing roses, violets and pansies
- tannery for turning cattle hides into leather
- main house
- grain was dried and stored in a granary
- A good water supply was important
- dairy
- baths
- cattle pens
- owner inspecting the farm with his manager

Exploring the effects of changing variables in simulations **Unit 4**

1. In a small group you are going to explore a CD ROM simulation. You will need to make a note of some of the choices you can make as you carry out your exploration. Your teacher will help you to find your way around the program.

2. Thinking about the type of choices you had to make when using the CD ROM simulation, try to design your own simulation. This could be about the Roman villa on page 46 or an idea of your own. You could think about exploring your bedroom at home or your classroom. You could design an adventure about a fantasy island or city or even driving a car or spaceship on a racetrack. Try to imagine someone using your program who is not familiar with that place.

Remember you need to think of all the choices that will be made and the things that will happen when you make those choices.

3. Share your designs with other groups and see if they understand what has to be done and whether they have any ideas about how you could improve your design.

Many rich Romans owned a villa in the country. This was both a holiday home and a working farm, surrounded by fields and gardens. The owner was often away, either on business or working at his job in a nearby town. When he was not there, a manager ran the farm and organised the slaves.

Unit 5.1 *E-mails*

18 Chelsea Street
Truro
Cornwall
TR4 6TJ
16 July 2000

Dear Amy

Thank you for your recent letter. It was great to hear from you. I have never had a pen friend before, so it is really exciting for me. I live in the country not far from the seaside. We only have one small shop in our village, which is where I usually buy my sweets and comics.

I love going down to the beach with my parents and our dog, Lucy. We usually go at the weekend. In the summer I go in the sea and I am getting much better at swimming now.

It gets busy here in the summer. Lots of holidaymakers from all over the world come to stay, which is good because I have plenty of other children to play with on the beach.

It is a bit quiet in the winter but there are still lots of things to do. I will tell you more about where I live next time I write and send you some pictures. Do write and tell me more about yourself and where you live.

From Jonah

Inbox

From: Jonah@compuserve.com

Sent: Tuesday, July 11 2000 8:25 am
To: amy@freeserve.co.uk

Hi. Thanks for the e-mail – great to hear from you.
I live in the countryside near the sea. We only have one shop, where I buy sweets and comics.
I go to the beach with mum, dad and Lucy (our dog!).
We usually go at weekends. In the summer I go in the sea. I'm getting much better at swimming.
It's busy in the summer – loads of holidaymakers from all over. It's great 'cos I have loads of friends to play with on the beach then.
It's quieter in winter, but still lots to do.
I'll tell you more next time I write and attach some photos for you.
Write and tell me more about you soon.

Jonah

Plan a letter to a pen pal using the template below. Think about the type of information they might want to hear from you, about where you live, what your school is like, your likes and dislikes.

Don't forget to ask some questions about them.

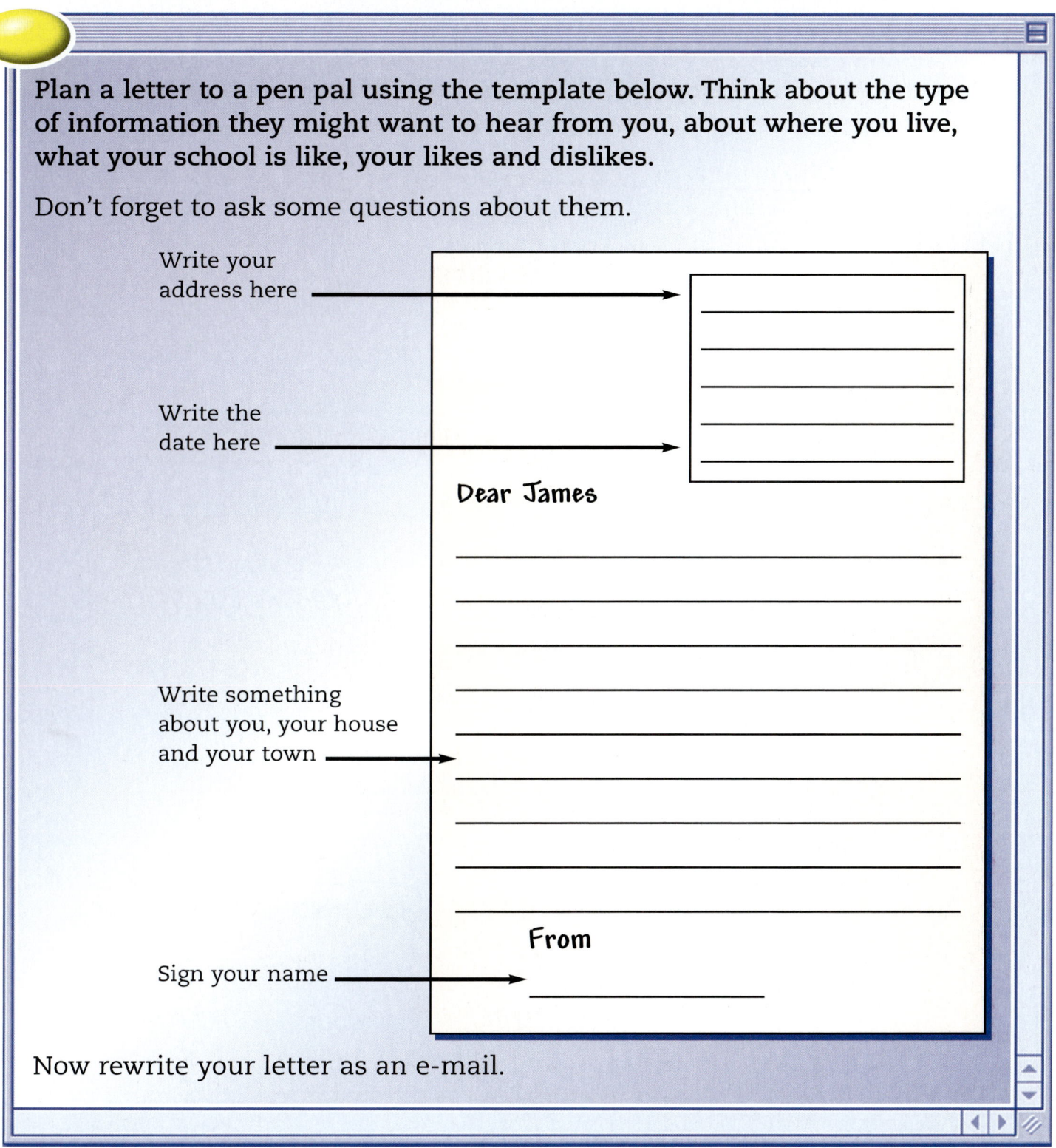

Now rewrite your letter as an e-mail.

Unit 5.2 E-mails

Look at the addresses below. Which are normal addresses and which are e-mail addresses? Can you match the pairs? Talk about the differences.

J. Samuels
The Teddy Bear Company
Worthing
Sussex
U.K.

ann@smart-learning.co.uk

francis@demon.co.uk

Francis Graham
49 Battersea Rise
London
SW18 7PD

CARA JENKINS
24 CARLTON WAY
CAMBRIDGE
CB4 8DW

jsamuels@teddybear.co.uk

Ann Griffiths
● SMART LEARNING ●
LIMITED
Sheraton House
Castle Park
Cambridge
CB3 0AX

carajenkins@freeserve.co.uk

Using an address book and adding attachments Unit 5.2

Can you change these addresses into possible e-mail addresses? The first one has been done for you.

John Wilkes
Supersavers
Brixton
London

johnwilkes@supersavers.co.uk

Hamid Jessop
Solva Infants School
Haverford
Wales

Sally Jones
St John's Primary School
Horsham
Surrey

Jackson Dunn
DEALS ON WHEELS
Hackney
North London

Joanne Collins
Superbooks Company
LUTON
BEDFORDSHIRE

Angela Foxton
Threemilestone Veterinary Surgery
Truro
Cornwall

51

Unit 5 E-mails INTEGRATED TASK

Inbox

From: paula&brendon@freeserve.co.uk

Sent: Monday, June 13 2000 12:31 pm
To: wendy@british-museum.ac.uk
Subject: School trip

We are planning a school trip and would like to know more about the British Museum. Please could you send us a copy of your brochure.

Thank you,

Paula and Brendon

Inbox

From: brian&kate@freeserve.co.uk

Sent: Sunday, Sept 21 2000 11:01 am
To: jonathan@museumnetwork.com
Subject: Scottish museums

Please could you send us information about museums in Scotland. Our class are planning a trip to a museum in the summer and we would like to know the choices.

Thanks,

Brian and Kate

Inbox

From: jack&nigel@freeserve.co.uk

Sent: Friday, Dec 19 2000 09:46 am
To: janemcdonald@londonzoo.com
Subject: Class project

We are doing a class project on endangered animals. Please could you send us any information about this, to help us with our project work.

Hope you can help!

Best wishes,

Jack and Nigel

Gathering, exchanging and developing information using e-mail **Unit 5**

Sending an e-mail is a quick and easy way of getting information.

With a partner you will be planning a message to send to someone to get some information. This might be about a trip you are going on with your class or for a topic you are working on at school.

Dear Class B

Thank you for all your e-mails. I hope the information we have sent you has been helpful. Look forward to seeing you on Thursday.

From: clare@londonzoo.com

Think about the questions you will ask and what information you will need. It is important to do this before you get to the computer so that you can make the most of your time.

You will need to have the e-mail address to put in the correct box of the message page. You might want to add this to your address book so that you can send another message later.

When you have returned from your trip you can send a thank you note and attach some of the work you have done after the visit. If there is something you were not sure about when you went on the visit you can ask about that too.

If you have time you can find other places to send messages to, and request information that will help with your work or with planning a visit.

Glossary

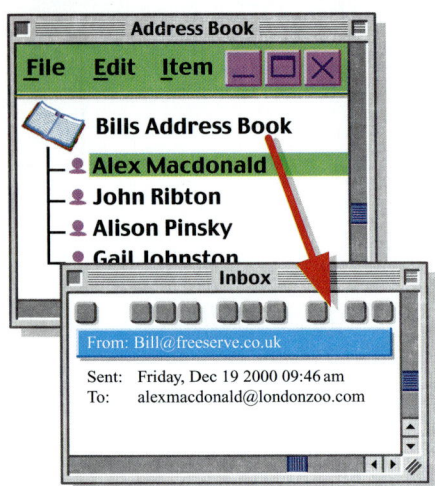

Address

Everyone on the Internet has an address that enables any other user to find them. (Every page on the World Wide Web also has its own address or URL.)

Address book

A software program that lets you keep your own file of names and e-mail addresses. You can type them in or copy them from e-mails that you receive.

Attachment

Any file from your computer that you attach to your e-mail. It can be text, pictures, sounds, cartoons, videos or photographs.

Backup

A copy of important data kept for safety in case the computer crashes.

Bookmark

See favourites.

CD ROM

A compact disk that can store large amounts of information that you cannot erase. ROM stands for 'read only memory'.

Clip art

Files of pictures in computer form that you can add to your documents.

Copy

Text and pictures can be copied to another area of the document or to a different document altogether. The copy facility is found under Edit.

Crash

This is the term used when the computer stops working and you are unable to retrieve all the information held.

Cut

Text and pictures can be cut from a document. This is usually done when you want the text or picture moved to another area or document. The cut facility is found under Edit.

Glossary

Data

When a computer is switched on, information (or data) can be stored in its memory. To keep the data safe, when the computer is switched off, you have to save it on the hard disk or a floppy disk.

Database

A system where files of information are organised and stored. A database can be searched for information quickly and easily.

Digital camera

A camera that you can plug into the computer to see the photographs you have taken on screen.

Drag

To depress and hold down the left mouse button while moving the mouse, to move an object on the screen.

DTP

Desktop Publishing is using a computer to design text and pictures for publications such as books, magazines and leaflets.

E-Mail

Electronic mail – used for sending messages on the Internet. Many people use e-mail to send letters more cheaply and quickly than normal mail.

Entry page

See Web site.

Favourites

A list you can keep on your computer of web pages that you like using or use a lot (also called bookmarks or short cuts).

Floppy disk

This can be used to save your data and store it safely, away from the computer.

Folder

A group of files stored together under the same name.

Fonts

You can choose from many different looking typefaces or fonts. There are thousands of different fonts, such as:

Times	Futura
Helvetica	Humanist
Garamond	Palatino

Glossary

Graphics

Pictures made or processed by a computer that can be taken from a clip art file or CD ROM.

Hard copy

Information from the computer printed onto paper.

Host

Any computer that is connected to the Internet is known as a host.

Hyperlink

Web pages are hypertext-linked. In a hypertext document there are certain icons and words, usually in colour and underlined, that are linked to other pages. If you select and click on one, a new page appears. Links that are live are called hyperlinks.

Icons

These are little pictures on the screen which represent some of the options you have. You can select icons using the mouse or keyboard.

Glossary

Interactive

When information is presented in an interactive way, you can click on buttons and choose the things you want to see and hear, using the mouse or keyboard. Hyperlinks make presentations interactive.

Internet

A worldwide network of computers and information. The Internet offers various services (or facilities) to anyone who is connected to it.

Internet Service Provider (ISP)

A company that provides you with a telephone link to the Internet.

Keyboard

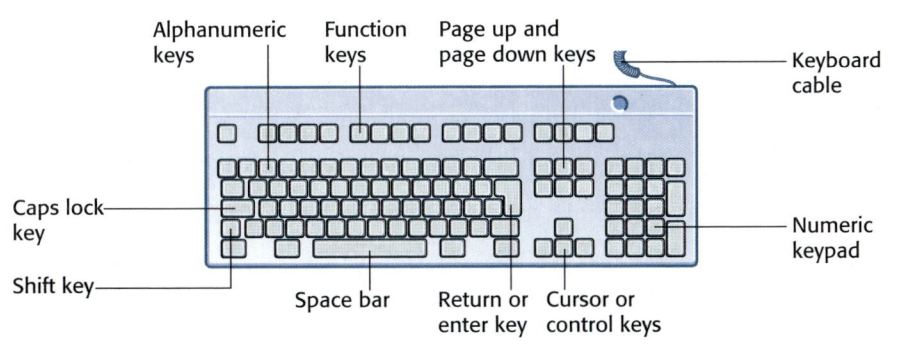

Memory

See RAM.

Menu

A list of available options.

Mouse

A device used to move a pointer around the screen and start a process by depressing a button.

Multimedia

To use computers to combine graphics, text, sound and video. Multimedia software usually comes on a CD ROM or DVD (digital video disk).

Network

A way of connecting two or more computers.

Paste

When you want to cut or copy text or pictures to other parts of a document, you use the paste facility to do so. The paste facility is found under Edit.

Procedure

A list of instructions, written in computer language, that can be given one name/command. When that name/command is given to the computer, the computer carries out the list of instructions.

Program

A set of instructions, written in computer language, for the computer to carry out particular tasks. Computer programs are pieces of software. The words and symbols used to write a program are called code.

RAM

This stands for Random Access Memory which is the type of memory chip used for the computer's main memory. Data held in it is lost when power to the computer is switched off.

Scanner

A machine that lets you copy pictures or words from paper onto the computer.

Glossary

Search box
Where you type the address of a website you want to visit.

Search engine
There are a number of programs found on sites that can be used to help you locate information on the Internet. These programs are called search engines, and there are two types: a directory and an index.

Software
A computer needs instructions in order to do anything useful. These instructions are called software and are always written in the form of programs.

Simulation
Computer simulations can represent real and imaginary situations and let you try things, or pretend to do something, that would be difficult or impossible to do in real life.

Spreadsheet
A model that you can use to help you make calculations and organise information, usually in number form.

Undo

If you make a mistake when you are amending a document, you can click on *undo* which will undo the last change or work done. This facility is found under Edit and also as an icon.

URL

Uniform Resource Locator – the way each address is written on the Internet so that everyone can find it (also called a web address).

e.g. an imaginary URL
http: //www.smart.com/index.html

↑ domain
↑ code
↑ page title

Web site

A set of web pages belonging to one address. Some web sites have a page to introduce the site called a entry page. Most have a page that links to all the main areas of the site called a home page.

WWW

World Wide Web – a collection of pages or sites that may contain pictures, sounds, cartoons and videos. The pages are written in hypertext so that users can move quickly from one page to another by means of hyperlinks. The World Wide Web lets you look at information from all over the world as is the most popular part of the Internet.

ICT wordsearch

In the grid below are 20 words – see how many you can find. If you need extra help use the glossary.

Words can run from left to right and right to left, across the grid, up or down the grid or in a diagonal line.

Look out for words that are back to front or upside down!

P	R	O	G	R	A	M	D	R	A	O	B	Y	E	K
N	O	I	T	A	L	U	M	I	S	A	D	D	P	T
T	P	P	I	U	Q	E	T	S	A	P	U	A	N	M
S	R	F	S	N	A	K	E	M	T	N	P	E	I	U
K	O	L	L	P	T	R	L	E	D	S	M	R	N	L
N	C	O	A	T	D	E	B	O	R	H	H	A	M	T
I	E	P	S	D	A	P	R	D	C	T	S	W	O	I
L	D	P	A	S	T	N	Q	A	T	C	N	T	U	M
R	U	Y	P	E	A	O	T	T	C	M	O	F	S	E
E	R	D	N	O	B	T	Z	A	P	T	C	O	E	D
P	E	I	G	R	A	P	H	I	C	S	I	S	N	I
Y	N	S	T	T	S	A	C	O	P	Y	A	V	P	A
H	E	K	P	R	E	R	I	N	T	E	R	N	E	T

Once you have completed the Wordsearch, you can use the glossary to find out what each word means.